Day Trading

The beginner's guide to making a fortune from day trading

By Sam Sutton

Table of Contents

Table of Contents 4

Introduction 1

Chapter 1: Preparing Yourself for Day Trading 2

Chapter 2: At the Beginning of Trading 8

Chapter 3: Techniques to Trade With 15

Chapter 4: Handling Your Money 23

Chapter 5: Becoming an Established Day Trader 30

Chapter 6: Things You Should Not Do While Day Trading... 38

Conclusion 44

Introduction

Congratulations on downloading your personal copy of *Day Trading*. Thank you for doing so.

The following chapters will discuss some of the many strategies you can use to be a successful day trader.

You will discover how important it is to make sure that you know how each of the strategies works and how they can help you achieve your goals.

The final chapter will explore some of the things that you should *not* do to be able to day trade successfully.

There are plenty of books on this subject on the market, thanks again for choosing this one! Every effort was made to ensure it is full of as much useful information as possible. Please enjoy!

Congratulations on downloading your personal copy of the *Day Trading*. Thank you for doing so.

Chapter 1: Preparing Yourself for Day Trading

Before you can even think about day trading, you need to make sure that you are fully prepared for the process. Day trading is not a technique or something that you can get involved in quickly, and it should be taken very seriously. It is not a get rich quick technique and something that you need to work at for a long time before you can do the best part of day trading.

There is no way that you can guarantee that you will be successful in day trading, but there are things that you can do to set yourself up for success so that you will not completely fail at the process. Nobody can see into the future when it comes to day trading (or anything, really), but there are things that you can do that will give you a better chance at being able to succeed with your day trading goals.

Try it Out

There is a saying that is nearly as old as time that goes "practice makes perfect." While there is no way to guarantee that you will be good at trading and the chances of being perfect are very low, you should still continue to practice. If you practice all of the time with your day trading, you will be able to learn the techniques that will later translate to you being successful with *real* day trading.

It is a good idea to try to find somewhere that you can practice. There are many websites that offer day trading practice for free. You won't make any money from the process, but you also will not have to spend any money because you will be able to truly just practice the day trading. There is no money that is involved with it, so you do not have to worry about losing anything. It will give you the chance to truly just practice when you want to learn more about day trading.

When you are practicing, you can get the help from expert day traders. This help can some from true professionals to everyone who does different things within the field of practice. The practice areas are a great place to find someone who can help you with day trading because the people who practice well are the ones who know what they are doing and they are wise for being able to practice the different things that they can do with day trading. It is a good idea to take the advice that they have to offer you. The day trading community is great at helping each other out, and it will allow you to see that there are many different options.

Think Short

Day trading is all about what you can make and sell

in a day. There is no day to day work that goes on with day trading, and that is one of the reasons that so many people enjoy the options that day trading has to offer people. When you want to make sure that you are doing different things with your day trading options, you must be able to do it within a day.

Look at the different things that day trading has to offer you *right now* and then figure out if that will be something that you can sell in the next day. At the close of business of the day that you have purchased your stock, you should make sure that you are going to be able to sell it. This is something that you need to do if you want to be successful at day trading. If you want to make sure that you are doing each of the different aspects of day trading, you need to be always prepared to go back to the day. At the end of each day, you should not have any stocks out or any that you are holding onto – instead, you need to make sure that you sell all of your stocks off at the end of the day.

Not Large

If you have invested in anything else in the past, you may notice that the day trading is much different than that. For example, with the other types of trading, you need to make sure that you are buying the largest and most valuable stock for the lowest amount of money. Day trading is not like that other than you will be spending the least amount of money possible. This means that you should try to find the stocks that are as low as possible and buy them for that reason. They need to be small stocks because you will need to get rid of them at the end of the day.

While you may not be able to make huge profits off of the smaller stocks as you would with larger ones, you will be able to buy more of the smaller ones and have more profits at the end of the day after you have already done what you needed to with the stocks that you are selling off. Just make sure that you get smaller ones so that it will be easier to offload them before the day is over.

You Will Lose

Anyone who goes into the game of *any* type of trading thinking that they are going to win at trades every time that they make one is simply a fool. There is no way to always win with the trading that you have, but you need to make sure that you are trying your best. Just always be prepared to lose because it can be disappointing to think you are going to make a ton of money with every single stock that you have and then have to deal with the problems that come along with not getting the most amount of money possible. You should be sure that you are working to make sure that you are getting the most out of the stock options and that you are going to be able to enjoy everything that the stock process has to offer you whether you are winning or losing.

If you keep your mindset the same and understand that you will lose sometimes, you will be less likely to get disappointed when you do lose money. It can *always* be a downer if you have never lost money on an investment before, but understanding that it *will* happen will ensure that you are not going to have to deal with all of the problems that come along with being down about the process. It can be much easier for you to try to deal with and to move on to be able to continue the investment process if you know that it is going to happen.

Before I continue any further I have some great news for you...

I just have to ask you a few questions before I tell you what it is just to make sure it's right for you.

1. Do you want to potentially make $5,000 per day, trading?

2. Are you willing to invest your time in learning the best ways to trade?

3. Do you want to live the life that can only be dreamt of?

If the answer to all of those questions is yes, then I have a treat for you which is ground breaking.

We have a free Forex course which virtually turns

anyone who has never traded ANYTHING in their entire life, into Forex market dominators overnight!

Now, you need to promise me one thing before I give you this course...

Please do not crash the Forex market. It is that powerful

Forex trading might have not been on your radar until today but the response of this course has been phenomenal.

If you get a chance to get it before I close the doors on this offer forever, remember me when you are on the top ;)

Join the rest of the traders who are living the life they always wanted and loving it:

http://www.trading-professionals.com/freecourse

Chapter 2: At the Beginning of Trading

How you do the first day that you are day trading can make or break your entire career. It can be a great idea for you to get started right away but make sure that you are truly prepared for the rest of the way that day trading works. It is a good idea to try to learn what you can before you get started, but even if you are unable to do that, there are quite a few things that you can do to ensure that you are getting a good start with trading.

Up to Date Trades

There are many ways that you can keep up to date with the stock market and with the different trades. As soon as you think that you are going to start day trading, start watching the market and keeping track of what is going on. By doing this, you will be prepared for the type of market that you are going to come into. Doing this will also give you an idea of what is going to happen with the different options when you get started. You need to make sure that is something that you are prepared for and that you are going to be able to get the most out of when you truly start with day trading.

One way that you can watch the stock market is by watching the news. You should have an understanding of the way that they work, and nearly every news network will publish the information about the stock market that you need to know. You can see whether it is going up or going down and whether you need to be prepared to sell a lot that day or not even get into the market for that particular day.

The other way that you can do this is using the power of the Internet. Most smartphones have applications that allow you to see the stock market. Even if you don't have a smartphone or only have access to a computer, you can use the Internet and watch the stock market. This is one of the easiest ways that you can figure out what you are doing and how much money you can make for that day.

Track Them All

When you are first getting started, you need to make sure that you are keeping track of all of the trades that you do. You need to make sure that you are keeping track of *all* of your trades, but the ones that you do at the beginning are especially critical. You need to make sure that you know what you are doing and what you are going to do in the future. Writing that information down is easy and will allow you to be able to look back on the record of what you made (including the mistakes that you made).

Some people choose only to write down when they have success, but that is not always the wisest decision. You should keep a log of all of the things that you did right in your day trading career. This can be everything from the way that you need to make sure that you are making money to all of the other options that are included with day trading. Write down when you make a lot of money, write down when you get a trade for a good deal and always write down the profits that you make each time that you make them. You will be able to look back on it and see what you did in the past. This is especially useful for you when you are struggling and want guidance to where you need to go again with your day trading career.

While you may want to write down the results (and the actions that you took to get there) when you do something good, you need to make sure that you are also writing down the mistakes that you made. Mistakes can be hard to own up to so writing them down in a log is one of the best ways to not make the same mistake again. Try to keep the log for the things that went the wrong separate from the things that went right so that there is never a question of whether you should do something again or not. The chances are, if it went south the first time that you did it, it would probably do so again.

Consistency is Key

As soon as you make the decision to day trade, stick

to it. This is why you need to make sure that it is something that you truly want to do when you first get started. It can be hard to be able to get to the point that you want and making sure that you make the decision to do it will allow you to truly be successful and get the most amount of money possible. It is always a good idea to stick with decisions that you have made and day trading is no different.

If you need to figure out what you are doing and where you are going to go with the different day trade options, you should make sure that you are getting the most out of the options that are included with the day trading that you have. It can sometimes be hard if you don't know what you are doing, but as long as you follow the steps that are required for getting started, you will be able to make sure that you are doing the most for the different parts of it. There are many different options that are included with day trading.

Being consistent with trading will allow you to make the most amount of money with your trades. Since you are buying and selling each business day, you need to make sure that you are stick to it day after day. There are many different things that go into day trading, and you need to make sure that you are consistent with the day trading options that you have so that you do not have to worry about keeping up with it or missing out on the stocks that could make you a lot of money.

Sam Sutton

Don't Be Shy

It is not uncommon for beginner day traders to get shy about what they are doing and the options that they have when it comes to trading. This is because they may be worried that they don't know what they are talking about or doing. There are many people who are more experienced than you on the day trading scene but do not let that hinder your ability to trade especially when you are first getting started.

If you see something that you want to buy because you think that it will be a lucrative option, buy it. The chances are that you will be pleased with the purchase that you make and it will make more sense for you to keep trading. If you are nervous about doing it, try it anyway so that you will be able to enjoy the stock without having to worry about any of the problems that come along with it.

This is a principal that goes hand in hand with understanding that you are going to lose sometimes. Take a look at stock, if you want to buy it, just buy it. If you find that you are not going to be able to sell it quickly, you may lose out on the money. That is the worst thing that can happen, though. If you find that you *can* sell it, you should just make sure that you are getting money from it. The best thing that can happen is that you will get a small profit from it which can allow you to make more money than what you were expecting to make from the stock.

Observe the Trades

Aside from the practice that is going to help you when you are learning about day trading and the different factors that go into it, you should also be observing people who have day trading experience. This means that you need to keep your eye out for professionals and for people who are doing a good job at day trading each time that they do it. Just make sure that you are getting what you can out of the day trading process and that you will be able to learn as much as you can from each of these people.

The people who are professional day traders are usually very open to the trades that they do. Watch them and see what they do. Learn their techniques and build your own off of them. You don't have to trade exactly like they do but learning the right way to do things will give you good options when it comes to your day trading career.

It may be more beneficial for you to make sure that you are trading the right way if you want to watch them first. Try to figure out *how* they are trading, take that into account and always do your best to provide yourself with the opportunity to do the same as them. Even if you don't have as much money to work with as the longstanding professional day traders, you can still use some of the techniques that they do. You don't even have to buy the same stocks as them as long as you are just making sure that you buy something that is similar and sells it in a way that makes sense for you and the options that you have when it comes to day trading. You can learn a lot from the professionals and model your professionalism off of theirs.

Chapter 3: Techniques to Trade With

Some people go into day trading blindly and think that they are going to be able to make money from the things that they are doing. This is not the case, and the chances are that you know this. Just because you are reading this book, it is easy to tell that you care about day trading and the different strategies that you can use to be successful. There is a lot more that goes into day trading than just hoping for the best and throwing your money around.

While, like everything with day trading, these things are not going to guarantee that you are going to win each and every time that you want to make a profit, following some of the strategies will help you to have a better time when it comes to making sure that you can truly benefit from day trading. You need to make sure that you can follow, at least, some of the strategies and that you will be able to get more out of them each time that you try different things. You never know what you are going to come across when it comes to day trading so knowing what your strategy will be for each thing that you come across can be helpful to you.

Economics of It

Trading is all about economics. You need to know what is in high supply (and will not cost you a lot) and what is in high demand (and will cost you a lot). If you can buy stocks that are in high supply at the beginning of the day and sell them off at the end of the day because they are in high demand, you will be better able to make sure that you are truly benefitting from the economic factors that come along with trading. It is a good idea always to try and make sure that you are getting the stock for the lowest amount possible and that you are selling it for the highest amount possible. This is the only way that you will be able to make a lot of money.

Knowing that the higher the demand, the higher the price is will help you to have an easier time when it comes to trading. You should make sure that you are only doing things that are in high supply when you first buy them. If you *do* find something that is in high demand and it is at a good price, snatch it up and then turn right around and sell it for higher. This is the best situation when it comes to day trading and one of the easiest ways that you can make a lot of money at once.

The Reward with the Risk

Similarly to how you need to make sure that you are comparing the demand and the supply of the stocks that you are purchasing, you need to compare the risk of the stock to the reward that you can get from it. This will also help you to decide how you are going to get the stock and how much it is going to work for you.

The risk is what happens when you are buying the stock. This is the amount of money that you can lose on the stock if it does not end up being one that you can win. You should always make sure that the risk is much smaller than the reward that comes along with the stock. This means that the amount of money that you could lose on it is smaller than the amount of money that you could make on it. This doesn't necessarily mean that you *are* going to lose money or make money on it, but it does mean that you need to be careful about the money that you are spending on different stocks.

On the other end of the spectrum, you should always look at the reward. Do you think that you will be able to sell it for double what you paid for it? While this isn't likely, it is a good way to look at the rewards that are associated with it. If the rewards seem like they are good and like they are something that you will be able to deal with in the long term, you need to take the stock and go with it. Even if you don't get the highest amount possible for the stock when you sell it toward the end of the day, you will be able to make some money from it.

Don't Put Your Eggs in One Basket

Always be careful when you are buying stocks. Even if you find a stock or any investment that seems is, you shouldn't spend all of your money on that one stock. Buy a few of them or even buy more than what you really think is necessary but then stop and move onto a different good stock that will allow you to make even more money. It is important that you do this so that you will be able to be safe with your stocks even if you don't have the right type of investment going on.

By trying out different stocks and making sure that you are investing your money in the right way, you will give yourself a chance to get even more money from the investments that you have made. This means that you need to be sure that you are getting a lot of different stocks that are in different categories and that will allow you the chance to try to do more with the options that you do have. It doesn't always have to be hard for people who are trying to get more out of the day trading options, but it is something that you need to make sure that you are doing the right way.

It can sometimes be hard for you when you are trying to find different stocks. You may not always be able to find exactly what you want, and the expected returns may not be the greatest, but it will be a way for you to make sure that you are going to have something different than one thousand dollars of the same things. If you try to find different stocks that are going to be profitable, you will be able to make money from them. You just have to try.

Different Types of Stocks

There are so many different types of stocks that you can invest in. The different investments will give you a chance to broaden the horizons of your portfolio and will give you a better chance at being able to sell off the ones that you have before the day is over. It can sometimes be complicated to learn all of the aspects of trading so make sure that you are doing it the right way and that you are going to be able to get the most out of it. If you work to make sure that you are getting the right type of stocks, you will have a much easier time when it comes to making money.

You will also be able to sell the stocks more easily. For example, you may struggle to sell 15 of the same stock because that is a big bulk sale. You probably won't struggle, though, selling 15 different stocks that all have different aspects to them. Just make sure that they are all profitable and that they are all going to bring of money that you want to be able to make.

If you can create a profile that is varied and different, you will have a better chance at selling the stocks and getting your money back for them when you are done with the process. It can sometimes be complicated to get the options that you have with selling stocks so make sure that you know what you are doing and that you are going to be able to include everything in the sale of the stocks that you do have. You may even be surprised that some people will want to buy all of the stocks that you have in your portfolio at the end of the day.

The First Hour

Similar to how the first part of your trading is the most important when you start to day trade, the first hour of the day is always going to be the most important part of the trading day. You need to make sure that you get to it early and that you buy your stocks as soon as you can. This is important for two reasons.

The first reason is that you will be one of the first people there and you will have access to the best stocks possible. There are many benefits that come with being the first to get to a specific trading option, but one of the biggest is that you will not have to compete with other people to be able to buy your stocks. You can get the best price possible, and you will have a handle on the day long before anyone else even shows up to buy stocks.

The second reason is that you will then have all day to sell off the stocks that you just bought. You need to make sure that you have as long as possible so that you don't have to worry about getting stuck with them at the end of the day (which is any day trader's worst nightmare). If you buy the stocks at the beginning of the day, you can then take the rest of the day and make sure that you are selling them so that you don't have to worry about having them left over. You will always have a fresh start.

Before I continue any further I have some great news for you...

I just have to ask you a few questions before I tell you what it is just to make sure it's right for you.

1. Do you want to potentially make $5,000 per day, trading?

2. Are you willing to invest your time in learning the best ways to trade?

3. Do you want to live the life that can only be dreamt of?

If the answer to all of those questions is yes, then I have a treat for you which is ground breaking.

We have a free Forex course which virtually turns anyone who has never traded ANYTHING in their entire life, into Forex market dominators overnight!

Now, you need to promise me one thing before I give you this course...

Please do not crash the Forex market. It is that powerful

Forex trading might have not been on your radar until today but the response of this course has been phenomenal.

If you get a chance to get it before I close the doors

on this offer forever, remember me when you are on the top ;)

Join the rest of the traders who are living the life they always wanted and loving it:

http://www.trading-professionals.com/freecourse

Chapter 4: Handling Your Money

Even people who are really good at managing their money and sticking to a budget may struggle when it comes time to be able to manage the different aspects of the trading process. This, when it comes to day trading. You need to try different things that will help you to save your money, and that will prevent you from spending too much money while you are trading the different amounts of money that you have. It is important that you work to make sure that you can use each of these things to make your trading experience more enjoyable.

The different monetary contingencies that you can put into place are all different and are all intended to be able to help you save money while you are making money. You can choose to use one of them or use them all, but they will help you while you are working on becoming a day trader. Just make sure that you know what you are doing and that you are using them in the proper way. Many of these contingencies are created for people who choose to automatically trade the different things that they have while they are buying and selling stocks during the course of a day.

23

Limiting Trades

There are some things that you will need to limit to be able to get the most out of the day trading process. For example, you may need to limit the number of times that you trade a certain stock, the amount of money that you put into one stock or the way that you can trade different things. By putting limits on everything that you have, you will be able to ensure that you are going to get the most out of the process and that you are going to be able to enjoy the benefits that come along with trading while you are still managing to save a lot of money on the different processes and on the different price points that you have in different areas.

You can choose to make your decision based on a single trade – for example, you can limit the number of times that you have put the one trade up or you can choose to do it with multiple ones. There are many different combinations that you can make with the trading process, and it is important that you include everything that you need with each of the different options that you choose to put on your limits. Each limit may have a different approach.

When you are setting up the limits that you have on things, you will need to either decide that you are going to do it manually or automatically. Manually will require you to review the process on a daily basis to make sure that you are not going too far above your limits. With the automatic limit setting, you will have limits that will be set ahead of time and will apply to all of the different trades that you do on a daily basis. The choice is yours and will depend on the way that you do things.

Budgeting

Creating a budget for your stocks and your day trading options is nearly the same as creating a budget in any other aspect of life. You need to decide how much you can afford to spend and what you are going to make. With day trading, you also need to figure out how much you are going to put into the trades on a daily basis. This is the limit that you want to be able to stick to each time that you do different trades and on a daily basis. It is important that you work to make sure that you are creating a budget that is completely reasonable for what you want to spend and what you could make throughout the day. You should be sure that you are going to get the most out of it by setting a budget that is reasonable for you.

As long as you are modest with your budget and you plan for any incidentals that could go on with your trades, you should have no problems sticking to the budget. It can be hard to be able to stick to the budget in your personal life, but it should be easy to do it when you are trading different things. As long as you know the amount that you want to spend on a specific day, you should always have a good idea of what that is going to mean for your business and your different trading options. Doing this will allow you to enjoy all of the benefits of trading without having to deal with the problems that come with reckless spending on investments.

Targeting for Price

You should always have an idea of how much each of the investments that are present in your portfolio should cost. This will help you with buying as well as selling and will give you all of the help that you need when it comes to the different options that are included in your portfolio. It is important to make sure that you are going to be able to make money back. If you don't know what something is going to cost you, you may struggle to figure out how much money you are going to get back for it.

Set a target for the price of a stock that you are going to buy. To do this, you must learn how much you want to be able to buy it for. Find out the value of the stock, the amount that you can get for it later on when you *do* decide to sell it and the average amount that it is going for. Stay within that target price. No matter what happens with your pricing options, make sure that you try to stick to the target price that you originally set. It may be hard to be able to get everything that you need out of it but knowing what your target price is should be enough to help you.

It is also a good idea to set a target price when you are selling your stocks. By knowing the value (and tracking it), you will be able to know what you want to get for it. If you try to sell it at any point throughout the day and you aren't going to be able to get the most amount of money for it, simply try later on in the day. Just be sure that you are not waiting too long to be able to get the money from it because you may end up missing out on the sale that you can get from the stock and you could end up with having the stock stuck in your portfolio at the end of the day so that you are unable to start the day with a clean slate like you are supposed to while you are day trading.

Stop Losses

If you have a stock that is eating up too much money or that is pulling out money from the amount that you want to be able to get, you can always put a stop loss on it. This means that it automatically gets cut off after you have lost a certain amount of money on the stock and that you don't have to worry about it draining anymore of the money that you have in your account. A stop loss is useful for people who use automatic stock options and who want to make sure that they are going to be protected if something would happen that their money is being drained by stock.

A stop loss is a great contingency to have in place if you are planning on doing automatic trading. This is not always the case for people who are new, so it is not something that you will probably need when you are first getting started but just be sure that you know that it is available. Once you start to use auto trading, you should always have a stop loss in place to cut off once you have reached a certain amount that is being taken for the stocks that you wanted to buy originally.

Available for Loss

Everyone sometimes loses when it comes to trading. The real question comes in how much you can lose and what you can do to get the loss out of the way of your trading. The loss is something that you need to be careful with but is also something that you will want to deal with as it comes. It can be helpful to set an "available for loss" balance that you are comfortable with losing.

By knowing the amount that you are comfortable with losing, it will make losses less of a shock to you and can make it easier for you to want to be able to continue trading even after you have started to lose money on the trade. There are many different options that you can set for your loss balance but usually keeping a set amount of money in your balance available to trade is the easiest way to do that.

Always protect your money when you are trading. The point of trading is to make money, and if you are unable to do that, you may not be able to get the most out of the trading process. You should have a good idea of what you have, what you want to be able to have in the future and every other aspect of trading. There are many different options that people who are trading may have to select and to make the right choice is always going to benefit you. It is good to make money, but it is even better to make sure that you are protecting the money that you already have. Losing is difficult, but it can be hard to rebuild money that you had in the beginning.

Chapter 5: Becoming an Established Day Trader

After you have learned all of the steps to go through getting started with day trading and the different processes that are associated with it, you should be able to easily become an established day trader. This doesn't necessarily mean that you will be as good as the people who have been doing it for years, but it does mean that you will be able to work toward making a career out of it. It is not uncommon for people who are working in the day trading field to completely replace their full-time income and to become someone who works for themselves and makes a fortune while doing so.

Financial freedom and stability are both possible once you have established yourself as a day trader and once you have made the decision to stick to it in a way that allows you to be as successful as possible. There are many different options that come along with day trading and making money is nearly always the result of following the right path toward success with day trading.

If you follow these ideas, you will be able to gain financial freedom as a day trader and become among the best people who trade.

Adapt to Flourish

There will be times when you must adapt while you are day trading. There may be things that you are not accustomed to, and there may even be things that you have never seen before. Be prepared for this and make sure that you can handle it. If you are prepared to adapt to everything that is going on with your day trading, you will know the right way to handle it and everything that needs to come along with day trading. There are many different options, and if you don't know the right way to do it, you may find that you are failing as a day trader. That is something you will not want after you have already established yourself as a trader.

Some things that can happen is that there may be unexpected huge fluctuations in prices, there may be problems with the system, and you may lose out on some of the stocks that you wanted. Don't let any of these things get in your way and don't let them bring you down. Just be prepared for them, and there will be no way that they can disrupt your day trading strategies.

If you are able to adapt, you will be great at day trading. You should make sure that you are always prepared for different things and that you don't have to worry about the problems that come along with trading. Day trading is all about being prepared to jump when you need to and that is one of the biggest problems that traditional investors have when it comes to day trading. They are used to having the chance to be able to take their time and figure out what they are doing.

Wait for It

Patience is huge when it comes to day trading. You may find that you have three or four days where you are not able to buy any quality stocks or make any investment. This is something that can be expected and something that you must be prepared for when you are day trading. The positive part of that is that when you have waited for a period to be able to get the trades that you want, you will be able to benefit from the trades that are much better than the ones that you passed up.

Having patience is important in any trading but is especially important in day trading. If you do not have patience and simply buy whatever stocks you want even if you think that they are not going to do well, you may end up with stocks that you cannot get rid of at the end of the day. The point of day trading is to start the next day with no stocks and nothing going on so that you can get a clean slate each time that you start your day.

Waiting for the right opportunity is a way for you to be able to get more out of day trading. It is something that you must be prepared to do and something that can be hard for some people – especially those who are used to not having to wait for anything. You need to make sure that you are trying y our hardest and that you are going to be able to enjoy the benefits that come along with day trading. If you don't have patience, you won't be able to enjoy any of the about because you will never be able to make a truly good deal.

Use Self Discipline

Having discipline can sometimes be hard when you are trying to make money. You may be tempted by the great stocks that you find even if you think that they are not a good price. This is something that can be detrimental to your career in day trading though because if you spend too much money on stocks and then lose all of that money, you won't have the chance to be able to invest more money and be able to make that money.

If you are disciplined with the money that you have, you will be able to save more of it. This means that you can put more money back to be able to invest in higher quality stocks and other investments. It also means that you will be safer if something happens to your trading and the money that you have. Just always be sure that you are going to be able to save money and that the discipline that you are doing is not something that is going to be detrimental.

By not having *too* much self-discipline, you are going to allow yourself to have the best chance possible. When you are day trading, it can be easy to get caught up and save too much money. This just means that you are keeping too much of it to yourself and not making the investments that you should be to be able to make a lot of money.

There is a delicate balance that lies between being self-disciplined and having too much self-discipline. Try to find that balance, keep it in your sights and always practice it so that you will be able to truly enjoy the process of day trading. It is not fun and there is no point in doing it if you are never able to make any actual money from it.

Past Experiences as Lessons

It is always a good idea to track your trades when you are first getting started, but it can also be beneficial when you are an experienced day trader, too. When you are able to make sure that you are working as a trader, you will benefit from understanding everything that you need to be able to get the most out of your trades. You can use these experiences that you had in the beginning as lessons later on in your trading career. It may seem like it is impossible for you to be able to get the most out of trading if you don't have anything to help you remember but it is a good idea to try to remember this information.

Keeping a log will help you remember what you did in the past that worked and what you did in the past that did not work. Understanding each of these things can make it easier for you later on. If you can keep track of what you spent, how much you invested and all of the options that were included with your spending on different things, you will have a better chance at working toward your goals.

The biggest aspect of trading is learning from your past experiencing. Figure out what worked for you, what didn't and what you can do in the future to make things even better for yourself. There are so many different options when it comes to trading so be sure that you keep track of these and of the options that are included. Write them down and keep them close so that you will always be able to reference them while you are trading.

Pocket that Cash

While you are trading, you should invest some of the profits that you make back into trading. This is the only way that you will grow in your business, and you will be able to improve your business in this way. If you are going to continue to do that, set aside a certain amount of profit to be able to invest back into trading. This is the easiest way for you to figure out how much you need to spend and how much you can afford to put back into your pocket.

It may take some time but you will eventually be profiting above the set amount that you wanted to be able to put back into the business. You should work hard to be able to include all of the different options that are with your trading business and to be able to get the most out of the trading experience. Try to pocket as much as you can after you have put it back. This can go toward your income.

The more that your pocket, the easier it will be for you to replace a full-time job with day trading. You will eventually get so good at day trading that you won't have to worry about working. This will be your income. You may even find that you are making more as a day trader and that you don't have to worry with everything that comes along with having a "real" job. Pocketing your money as much as possible is the first step to building your fortune with day trading and giving yourself the financial freedom to live life the way that you want to.

Before I continue any further I have some great news for you...

I just have to ask you a few questions before I tell you what it is just to make sure it's right for you.

1. Do you want to potentially make $5,000 per day, trading?

2. Are you willing to invest your time in learning the best ways to trade?

3. Do you want to live the life that can only be dreamt of?

If the answer to all of those questions is yes, then I have a treat for you which is ground breaking.

We have a free Forex course which virtually turns anyone who has never traded ANYTHING in their entire life, into Forex market dominators overnight!

Now, you need to promise me one thing before I give you this course...

Please do not crash the Forex market. It is that powerful

Forex trading might have not been on your radar until today but the response of this course has been phenomenal.

If you get a chance to get it before I close the doors on this offer forever, remember me when you are on the top ;)

Join the rest of the traders who are living the life they always wanted and loving it:

http://www.trading-professionals.com/freecourse

Chapter 6: Things You Should Not Do While Day Trading

Now that you know all of the things that you *should* do while you are day trading, you need to take a look at some of the things that you should be avoiding while you are day trading. Doing any of these things can hinder your ability to make money while you are trading and can cause major problems for you if you try to do them. They will not always destroy your day trading business but they have the potential to do so if you are not able to avoid them. Since it can be detrimental to your business, you should always try your best to stop these things before you even have a chance to start them.

Focus on One Strategy

Strategies are great and you absolutely need to have one if you are going to be trading but not having more than a single strategy can be detrimental in the event that you are not able to use that strategy. You should always make sure that you are working your hardest to build up many different strategies and that you are going to be able to do more with what you have. It can be hard to find more than one strategy that works for you and your business but if you are able to find one then you will be able to find more than one.

By allowing yourself to try different methods of trading, you will have more of an opportunity at getting the results that you want. This means that you need to make sure that you are learning as much as possible and that you are going to be able to try different things out. It can be complicated if you do not know what you are doing, but the easiest way to get started with methods of trading is to simply have a backup plan that you can use if your original trading plan does not go the way that you want. The backup plan with is your first alternative.

From there, you can learn even more methods of day trading. Fast selling, wait and watch approaches and trial and error are all a few different ways that you can make sure that you are getting the best experience possible when it comes to the various methods of trading.

Sit Back

Do not ever take a passive approach to trading. You should always be aggressive about your trades, make sure that you are doing everything that you can to be able to get the results that you want and always go after every single one of the trades that you are hoping for. It is a good idea to try different things to get there but don't sit back and wait for those to come to you. It will not only be detrimental to your efforts when it comes to trading but it can also be detrimental in that there are many different options that you can be missing out on.

If you are passive about the trading process, you will miss out on trades. There are no other traders who are successful and took a passive approach. It simply will not happen. Even when you are first getting started, it is important that you try to be as aggressive as possible so that you can get the results that you want. It makes more sense to push to get what you want than to sit and wait for it to just come to you. Trades don't work like that, and there is no magical way for you to get all of the stocks that you want – you have to put in the work and, sometimes, fight to be able to get them.

Do Too Much Effort

There is no reason that you should ever put more than a few hours on getting a stock. As a day trader, that is probably around 10% of your total day that you have available to trade. You don't want to waste it just chasing one thing and there are many different reasons that you may not want to continue chasing that one trade. One of the biggest reasons is that there is no guarantee that you are going to get a lot of money from it or that it will be profitable at all. There are too many other stocks that are available to you for you to waste all of your time on just one of them. It is important that you work toward getting different ones.

If you find that you have wasted too much time on

one stock or one investment, you will not be able to get that time back, but you can try to make up for it by working twice as quickly at the other trading options. This means that you will sometimes need to double down your speed and not waste any time at all on the various trades. It also means that you can sometimes invest in trades that are going to be really bad for your overall profit. It is often just easier to chalk it up to a bad day and move on until the next day. If you can sell the stock that you wasted too much time on, that is beneficial and will allow you to, at least, recoup some of the money even if you can't get the time back.

Rely on Others

Nobody is going to hold your hand when it comes to trading. You need to make sure that you are working for yourself and that you are learning everything that you can on your own. While it is great to have the ability to learn from people who have come before you, they are not going to be the ones who show you what they can do. You need to learn the right way to do it all yourself and to get the most out of the experience of day trading. There are many different ways that you can teach yourself.

Don't rely on others. Rely only on yourself to make sure that you are going to be able to be the best at day trading. Reading this book is one of the easiest ways that you can start out your independent day trading career. Just reading this book is going to give you a great start and will allow you to see that you are truly going to be a great day trader. There are so many options from here that you can take your day trading career to the next level. It is important that you learn the right way to do it.

Stop Trading Out of Fear

If you don't take chances in trading, you will truly struggle to get to where you want to be. You need to take chances at not be afraid to trade something even if it seems like it is going to be a big risk. By allowing yourself the chance to see that good thing can come out of risky trades, you will be getting the upper hand when it comes to your day trading experience. There are many different options that you can enjoy but you will miss out on all of them if you are afraid to take a chance.

For this reason, it is important to weigh the benefits and the risks of trading. You need to figure out what is going to work for you and what is not going to work for you. If it seems like the trade that you are going to be making is going to be a huge risk, you may want to reconsider it. Always weigh the pros and the cons of a trade but also try to do some things that will scare you.

All in all, trading is a risk. You need to decide which smaller risks are things that you want to do and if they are worth it for your personal day trading career.

Day Trading

Conclusion

Thank for making it through to the end of *the name of the book*. Let's hope it was informative and able to provide you with all of the tools you need to achieve your goals of

The next step is to explore all of the practice options for day trading and put your dreams into actions. You will soon be making a fortune day trading.

Finally, if you found this book useful in any way, a review on Amazon is always appreciated!

Before I let you go and make a lucrative amount of money using this information I would like to share something with you...

I just have to ask you a few questions before I tell you what it is just to make sure it's right for you.

1. Do you want to potentially make $5,000 per day, trading?

2. Are you willing to invest your time in learning the best ways to trade?

3. Do you want to live the life that can only be dreamt of?

If the answer to all of those questions is yes, then I have a treat for you which is ground breaking.

We have a free Forex course which virtually turns anyone who has never traded ANYTHING in their entire life, into Forex market dominators overnight!

Now, you need to promise me one thing before I give you this course...

Please do not crash the Forex market. It is that powerful

Forex trading might have not been on your radar until today but the response of this course has been phenomenal.

If you get a chance to get it before I close the doors on this offer forever, remember me when you are on the top ;)

Join the rest of the traders who are living the life they always wanted and loving it:

http://www.trading-professionals.com/freecourse

Description

Financial freedom is possible when you learn the right way to day trade. There are things that you can do that will help you to make a fortune and ways that you can enjoy the benefits that come with working for yourself. Learn about day trading and get a feel for the industry.

You will be able to benefit from everything that day trading has to offer when you learn the basics. The strategies will allow you to learn the right way to day trade and to be able to start making money. Learn what you can about day trading right now and you will be able to get more out of the experience.

Read on to find out all of the different ways that you can benefit from day trading, how you can make the most out of your day trading career and what you should look out for before you start to do your day trading experience. The book includes everything that you need to know to get started.

This is just the beginning, though. Once you have learned the basics that are covered in this book, you can take your day trading experience and run with it. The options are limitless and so is the amount of money that you can make. You will soon be making a fortune with everything that you have learned in this book and about day trading. Financial freedom is in your future!